AN
EASY-READ
FACT
BOOK

Cars

Michael Jay

Franklin Watts
London New York Toronto Sydney

© 1982 Franklin Watts Ltd

First published in Great Britain in
  1982 by
Franklin Watts Ltd
8 Cork Street
London W1

First published in the USA by
Franklin Watts Inc.
730 Fifth Avenue
New York
N.Y. 10019

UK ISBN: 0 85166 957 3
US ISBN: 0-531-04445-9
Library of Congress Catalog Card
  Number: 82-50063

Printed by Cambus Litho,
  East Kilbride, Scotland.

Photographs supplied by
Popperfoto
David Jefferis

Illustrated by
Jim Dugdale
Christopher Forsey
Hayward Art Group
Michael Roffe

Designed and produced by
David Jefferis

Technical consultants
Ronald Barker
Mel Nichols

AN EASY-READ FACT BOOK

Contents

The first cars

In 1769 a French engineer, Nicolas Cugnot, built a three-wheeled steam-powered truck. His machine was the earliest ancestor of the motorcar. It was designed as a gun carriage for the French army. It could move at only 3 mph (5 km/h) and had to stop four times an hour to build up steam in its boiler. Other "steamers" were tried in the nineteenth century, but they were slow and clumsy.

One of the first practical cars with a gasoline engine was made by a German, Karl Benz, in 1885. It looked very different from a modern car, with three spidery wire-spoked wheels and a bar to steer with.

Early motoring was dirty, drafty and unsafe. In 1903 a Winton car was driven from San Francisco to New York. The 4,500-mile (7,200-km) journey took 65 days, of which more than 20 were spent making repairs!

△ This advertisement dates from 1905. The American company Oldsmobile made only 433 machines in 1901.

▽ Before 1908 cars were hand-built and expensive. The Ford Model T was the first car to be made on an assembly line. In 1909 over 10,000 Model Ts were sold. By 1927, when Ford finally stopped making the car, over 15 million had been made.

Parts of a car

The human body is made of various "standard" parts – the head, hands, feet and so on. In much the same way the car is made of seven basic systems.

The engine is the heart of the car. It is controlled by a floor-mounted accelerator pedal.

The transmission links the engine to the drive wheels, which may be at the back, the front, or sometimes both.

The steering is a rod-and-lever system that turns the front wheels.

The electrical system consists of a large battery which provides power to start the engine and to work all the electrical equipment.

The brakes are controlled by a floor-mounted footpedal. An emergency brake is used for parking.

The suspension uses springs and shock absorbers to cope with bumps.

The body is usually made of pressed steel parts welded together.

▷ This Austin Metro is a typical small modern car. It has front-wheel drive and can seat four to five people in comfort – all in a body just 11 ft 2 in (3.4 m) from bumper to bumper.

Engine mounted sideways to save room

Battery

Brakes. One unit for each wheel.

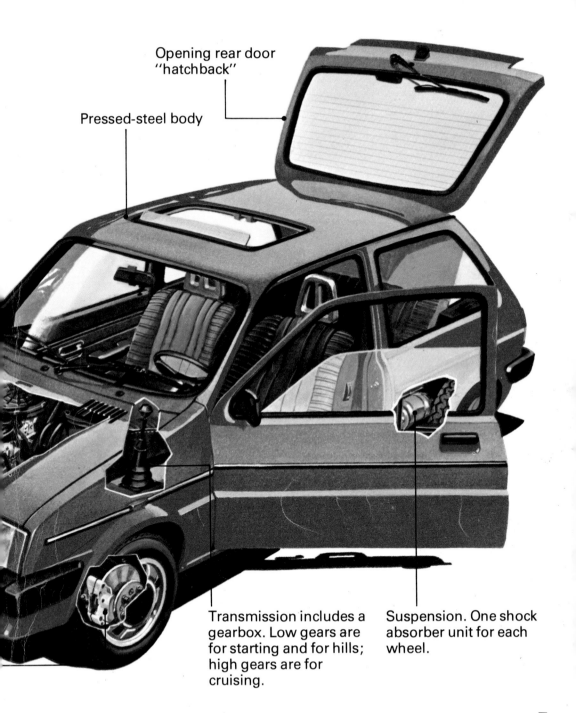

Opening rear door "hatchback"

Pressed-steel body

Transmission includes a gearbox. Low gears are for starting and for hills; high gears are for cruising.

Suspension. One shock absorber unit for each wheel.

7

Inside the engine

△ Here you can see some of ways in which the engine and driving wheels can be arranged. Front engine/rear drive used to be the most popular. Most new cars have the front-engine/front-drive arrangement.

The engine is the source of a car's power. Inside it are several pistons, like the one shown on the right.

Each piston moves up and down in a cylinder. Fuel, a mixture of gasoline and air, is sucked into the top of the cylinder. An electric spark plug provides a powerful flash of electricity. This makes the fuel mixture explode. The explosion forces the piston down the cylinder and turns the crankshaft through a connecting rod.

The turning of the crankshaft is measured in rpm – revolutions· per minute. At cruising speed in a medium-sized family car, the crankshaft will be revolving nearly 50 times *every second*!

The crankshaft is connected to the gearbox, which transfers the engine's power to the driving wheels.

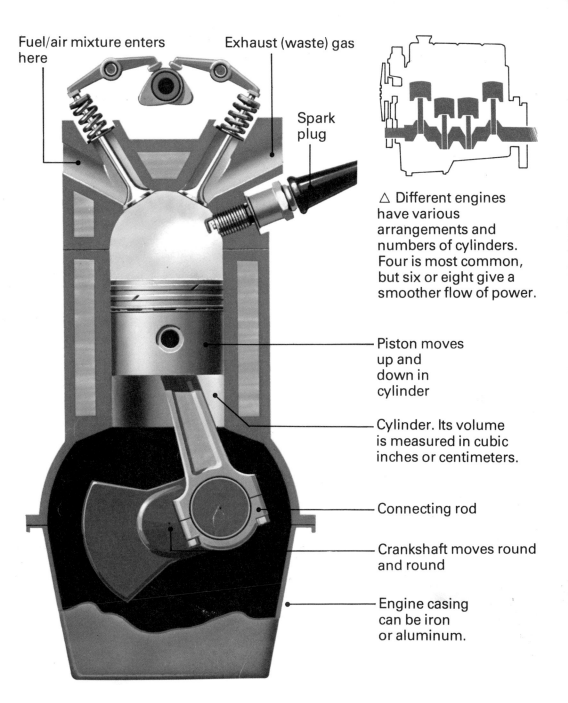

Fuel/air mixture enters here

Exhaust (waste) gas

Spark plug

△ Different engines have various arrangements and numbers of cylinders. Four is most common, but six or eight give a smoother flow of power.

Piston moves up and down in cylinder

Cylinder. Its volume is measured in cubic inches or centimeters.

Connecting rod

Crankshaft moves round and round

Engine casing can be iron or aluminum.

Car design

Car styling is the art of designing a vehicle so that it looks appealing. Good-looking cars tend to sell better than ones that are not attractive.

Styling fashions have changed over the years. In the 1920s and 1930s long hoods and fenders were popular. In the 1950s big rear fins and lots of shiny chrome trim were in demand. Today cars are lower and sleeker than ever before. Smooth, flowing lines cut down air drag.

▷ This Duesenberg shows the "big car" fashion of 1929. It has an open front area for the chauffeur, like the hansom-cab arrangement of the 19th century.

▽ The 1982 Toyota Celica is carefully styled to reduce air drag. Most new designs have a similar sloping nose section.

Rear deck opens up as a "hatchback" door

Covered steel wheels replace the spokes of earlier years

Tinted windows

Headlights follow shape of nose

Rubber bumper absorbs small knocks without any damage

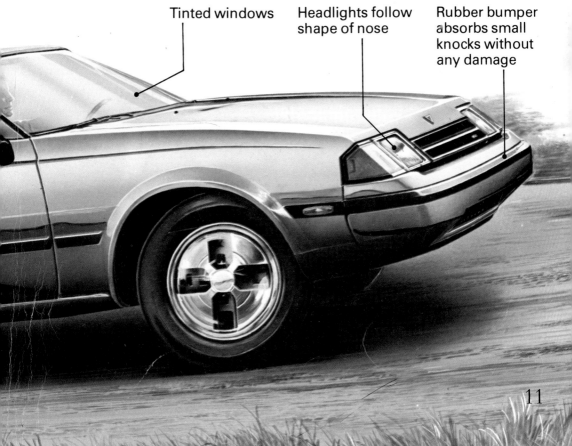

Safety

△ This Citroen GSA has a very good active safety feature. If a front tire blows out, the car will not pull sharply to one side. It can be steered safely until brought to a halt.

The first motoring accident was in 1771 when Cugnot drove his steam truck into a wall in Paris. Since then, the accident rate has climbed to very high levels. In 1969, the worst year so far, 56,400 people were killed in car accidents in the USA alone.

Cars are now designed with important safety features. Many of these are built into the car. All new car bodies have strong roofs and doors. Front parts of some cars crumple when a crash occurs. Windshields are also designed to keep people from flying out. Steering wheels sometimes collapse, preventing injury to the driver.

Automobiles are designed with good brakes, steering, and road-holding ability. Tires are designed to hold to roads and to wear a long time. Seat belts, when worn, can stop people from smashing through windows.

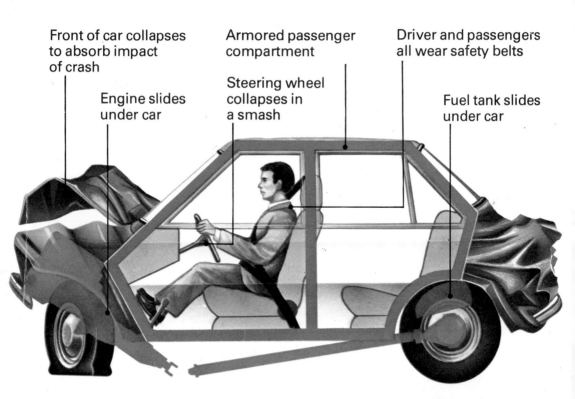

Front of car collapses to absorb impact of crash

Engine slides under car

Armored passenger compartment

Steering wheel collapses in a smash

Driver and passengers all wear safety belts

Fuel tank slides under car

△ This car shows several safety features, including an engine and fuel tank which slide under the passengers instead of crushing them.

▷ This accident is typical of the thousands which happen every day across the world. In 1975 world deaths from road accidents passed the 25 million mark.

Great cars of the past

Very few cars have just the right combination of style, performance, comfort and reliability to become all-time greats. Here are five examples, each with its own character.

▽ Rolls-Royce Silver Ghost, 1906. The first really smooth and reliable car.

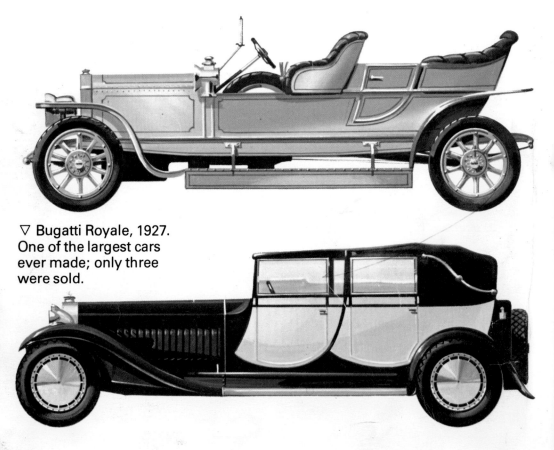

▽ Bugatti Royale, 1927. One of the largest cars ever made; only three were sold.

▽ Mercedes-Benz SSK, 1929. Racing versions were still winning nine years later.

▽ Cord 812, 1937. A very advanced car for its time, it had front-wheel drive.

▽ Jaguar XK 120, 1948. Its engine design is still used in some Jaguars today.

City cars

Everyone is familiar with snarled-up city traffic. Long traffic jams build up in the rush hour and parking spaces are hard to find. Pollution from exhaust fumes can be a hazard too. Traffic police in Tokyo have to wear face masks and carry oxygen bottles in case they need fresh air. Despite all this, many people prefer to use their cars instead of public transport in big cities.

△ Mid-morning traffic on a quiet day in London. In rush hours the traffic barely moves.

▷ Four good town cars. All are comfortable, use little fuel and are compact so they can fit into tight parking spaces.

△ Lincoln/Mercury Lynx, the US luxury version of the Ford Escort. The Escort is made and sold all over the world.

△▽Renault Le Car. In Europe this is simply known as the Renault 5. The Fiat Panda below is of similar size.

△ The Honda City is one of Japan's city cars. It comes with a tiny motorbike which folds neatly into the rear load area.

17

Racing cars

The history of motor racing is almost as old as motoring itself. The first real race was held in France in 1895. The winner achieved an average speed of 15 mph (24 km/h) over a 732-mile (1,178-km) course from Paris to Bordeaux and back.

In these early years there were sometimes cars with electric, steam or gasoline engines, all competing in the same race. This would not be possible today, for there are many different kinds of racing. Each race has its own strict set of rules.

This set of rules is known as the formula. This gives the size of engine to be used, the weight of the car, the amount of fuel to be carried, right down to the tiniest detail.

The formulas for all motor sport would fill a book, but the best known is that of the World Championship, Formula One.

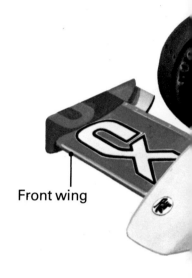

Front wing

△ This Formula Atlantic U2 racer has many design features to be found on other racing cars. The front and rear wings do the opposite job to those on an aircraft. The U2's wings lift *downwards*, and keep the car firmly on the track.

Wide wheels and tires for maximum grip on track

Engine mounted behind driver

Lightweight streamlined body

▽ The Bugatti T35 was the most successful racing car between 1924 and 1930. It was widely sold to amateur drivers and won more than 1,000 races.

Dragsters

Dragsters race in pairs in a straight line down a quarter-mile (402-m) strip. The kings of the strip have hurtled down that short distance in just 5.637 seconds, while the top speed stands at an amazing 255.58 mph (411.31 km/h).

Dragsters come in different shapes and sizes. The fastest cars with ordinary engines are the AA fuelers. These run on a mixture of alcohol and nitromethane. This mixture gives their engines twice the power of a "gasser," a gasoline-fueled dragster. The newest and fastest dragsters are powered by jet and rocket engines.

In the USA there are over 500 drag strips.

Support rod for body

Specially made tires

△ This is a Funny Car, one of the various types of dragsters. Funny Cars have bodies styled after those of real production cars.

▽ Here you can see what happens during the few seconds of a dragster's race.

The soft rubber tires smoke as the cars start

Cars accelerate, aiming for top speeds of over 250 mph (400 km/h)

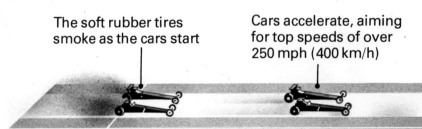

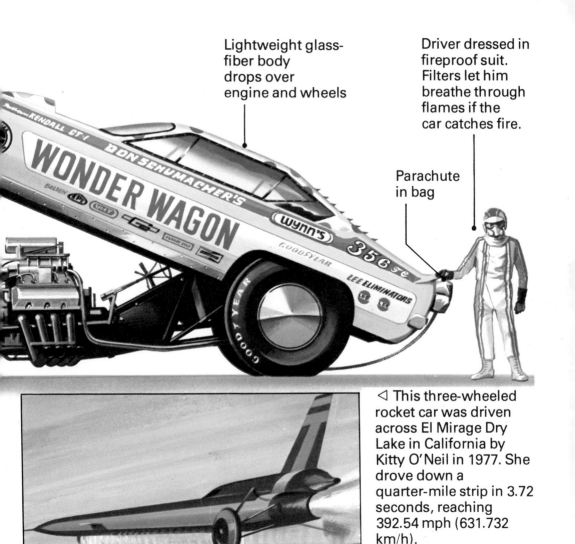

Lightweight glass-fiber body drops over engine and wheels

Driver dressed in fireproof suit. Filters let him breathe through flames if the car catches fire.

Parachute in bag

◁ This three-wheeled rocket car was driven across El Mirage Dry Lake in California by Kitty O'Neil in 1977. She drove down a quarter-mile strip in 3.72 seconds, reaching 392.54 mph (631.732 km/h).

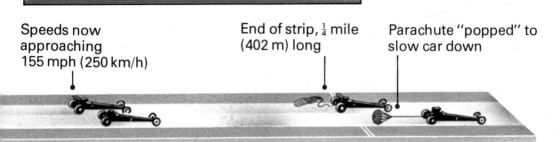

Speeds now approaching 155 mph (250 km/h)

End of strip, ¼ mile (402 m) long

Parachute "popped" to slow car down

21

Land speed record

△ This Gobron-Brillié roared along at over 103 mph (166 km/h) at a race meeting in Belgium in 1904.

The first land speed record holder was Frenchman Gaston de Chasseloup-Laubat. In 1898 he drove his electric car at 39.24 mph (63.14 km/h) to start a long history of record-breaking.

Cars with huge piston engines drove speeds up until jet and rocket power took over in the 1960s. Since 1970 the official record has stood at 622.287 mph (1,001.473 km/h), held by Gary Gabelich in his rocket-powered Blue Flame. The car burned hydrogen

peroxide and natural gas. The mixture burns with an intense blue color, hence the car's name.

Since then, Stan Barrett has gone faster. His Budweiser Rocket broke the sound barrier in 1979, adding another 117 mph (188 km/h) to Blue Flame's speed. The run, at Edwards Air Force Base in California, was not officially timed however, so Blue Flame remains the holder of the "official" land speed record.

△ Blue Flame made its runs on Bonneville Salt Flats in Utah, USA. Practically all recent attempts have been made on these flat salt plains.

Computers at the controls

△ The computer car of the future will be fully automatic. Once you have fed in route instructions, a computer will take over, using guide wires sunk into the road to find its way.

Cars today already include lots of computer equipment. Electronic ignition systems improve first-time starting. Trip computers display the fuel consumption, average speed, the time that the journey will take and other useful information. Many cars have robot "watchdogs" aboard. These indicate if doors are unlocked, seat belts are undone, brakes are worn.

In the near future radar units will be built in to probe the road ahead in thick fog to warn you of obstacles. The radar unit may even take over the brakes to avoid a collision.

Japanese car makers are making voice displays. Using a micro-chip to produce robot speech, these instruments simply *tell* you what is wrong.

Many of these things have been possible for some time, but only now can they be made in a cheap, reliable and small enough form.

△ The trip computer is plugged into the car's vital systems so it can provide the information you ask for.

▷ Car thefts could be harder if these door locks catch on. You punch in your secret number to open the door.

△ This small color TV shows useful information at the touch of a button.

△ This may be the look of a future car's instrument panel. Glowing light displays and voice warning units give the driver information.

Saving fuel

▽ This car includes many of the features which car designers are planning for their future models.

The race to save expensive fuel is producing a new range of sleek and smooth cars. Streamlined body shapes slip through the air more easily than upright, boxy ones – and this saves fuel. The vehicle shown below, if built, would need less than half the power of

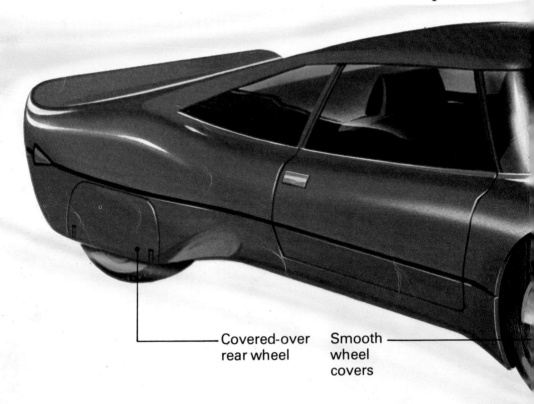

Covered-over
rear wheel

Smooth
wheel
covers

a present-day car to cruise at 62 mph (100 km/h).

Air drag is measured in Cd. The worst possible shape, a square box (like a truck), has a Cd of 1.0. The best possible shape (like a teardrop) has a Cd of 0.1. Most new cars have a Cd around 0.4, but it should not be too difficult to reduce this to 0.2.

Other fuel-saving measures include engine improvements and changes in tire design.

△ This car's hood is covered with wool tufts for wind-tunnel testing. The tufts should all blow smoothly back if the designers have done their work correctly.

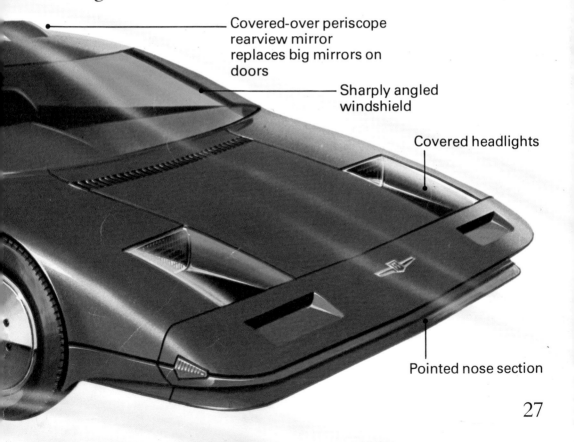

Covered-over periscope rearview mirror replaces big mirrors on doors

Sharply angled windshield

Covered headlights

Pointed nose section

27

New sources of fuel

▽ This picture shows two cars at an automatic fueling station in the year 2000. The small electric car is having its battery pack changed. The large cruiser is being topped up with LH2.

Oil shortages and rising prices are making scientists look for new ways to power road vehicles.

For short distances small electric runabouts may be useful. Making batteries that are powerful enough has been a problem, but improved types are being developed. Electric cars will

be quiet and almost pollution-free.

Long-distance motoring needs another solution. Synthetic fuel made from coal is already used in South Africa, and other countries will follow. It is expensive though, so fuel containing alcohol, made from plants like trees and desert shrubs, may be better.

Some researchers think that liquid hydrogen (LH2) may be the answer. Available in huge amounts from water, LH2 may be the ultimate pollution-free fuel.

Glossary

Here is a list of some of the technical words used in this book.

Accelerator
Floor-mounted pedal. When pushed by the right foot, it increases the speed of the engine.

Cd
Coefficient of drag. The term describes how easily any particular shape goes through the air. Bad shapes are boxy and upright. Good shapes are smooth and sleek, like teardrops.

Formula
Set of rules for each type of motor racing. The best known is Formula One. The winner of this race becomes the world champion racing driver.

Liquid hydrogen (LH2)
At present used as a fuel in rockets like the Space Shuttle. LH2 is super-cooled hydrogen gas, which can be extracted from water. At $-418°F$ ($-250°C$) it forms a liquid, but storage in cars is a problem. Despite this, some scientists think it will make a good replacement for gasoline.

Piston
Part of the engine which goes up and down inside the cylinder. The bottom of the piston connects with the crankshaft.

Radar
Electronic system which uses reflected radio wave "echoes" to detect obstacles ahead. These can penetrate the thickest fog.

Safety features
Good steering, braking, road-holding and other features built in to a car. These help the driver to safely avoid a dangerous situation.
   Built-in safety adds protective features to the car such as a strong passenger "cage" to protect the people inside if an accident happens.

Sound barrier
Breaking the sound barrier means going faster than the speed of sound. This changes

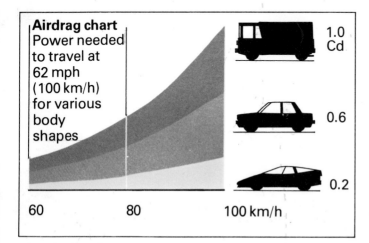

Airdrag chart
Power needed to travel at 62 mph (100 km/h) for various body shapes

1.0 Cd

0.6

0.2

60   80   100 km/h

with height and temperature. At sea level it is about 761 mph (1,225 km/h), but gradually decreases with height to 660 mph (1,062 km/h).

Synthetic fuel
A type of liquid extracted from coal, used as a replacement for gasoline. Other synthetic fuels can be made from plants and trees.

Transmission
The parts of a car which join the engine to the drive wheels. It includes the gearbox and propeller shaft.

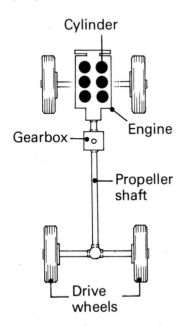

Car registrations

Each country has its own set of letters, which must be displayed on any car going to another country. They are normally shown in oval plates like the ones below.

A	Austria
AUS	Australia
B	Belgium
CDN	Canada
CH	Switzerland
D	West Germany
DK	Denmark
E	Spain
F	France
GB	Great Britain
GR	Greece
H	Hungary
I	Italy

IRL	Ireland
L	Luxemburg
N	Norway
NL	Netherlands
NZ	New Zealand
P	Portugal
S	Sweden
SF	Finland
SU	USSR
TR	Turkey
USA	United States
YU	Yugoslavia
ZA	South Africa

Index